The Texture Of Being

UNDERSTANDING YOUR TRUE SELF

by

Roy Whenary

LOTUS HARMONY PUBLISHING

Devon, England

First published in Great Britain in 2002
by LOTUS HARMONY PUBLISHING
Foxhole, Dartington, Totnes, Devon, TQ9 6EB

website: www.lotusharmony.co.uk

Copyright © 2002 Roy Whenary

Cover photo by David Cowell
(Digital Arts/Dartington)

Logos by Gordon Stowell

ISBN: 0-9543100-0-4

Dedicated
to the life and teachings
of Jean Klein

Acknowledgements

Firstly, I would like to acknowledge the friends who were kind enough to read the first draft of this book: Alan Jacobs, Jamie Haley, Jeremy Sellars, John Liddle, Daniela Coronelli and Diana. Your comments were invaluable and your encouragement gratefully received.

I would also like to thank Gordon Stowell for the Lotus Harmony logos, David Cowell for his superb photograph and Eddie Shapiro for his encouragement and support.

Special thanks to Movement Teacher Daniela Coronelli, as it was in her class that the title for the book spontaneously appeared - and to Eddie Shapiro, who suggested the sub-title.

Contents

Foreword

THE TEXTURE OF BEING is a profound insight into the human dilemma. We all wish to be happy - and, for many, that might simply mean to survive in this mad, mad world, where we can go to the moon and yet cannot solve our own personal and political problems.

We perpetuate suffering in the process of creating a comfortable life for ourselves. We want happiness, which for many of us means having and gathering more. But what we really want is to have a good life, to have a sense of physical and material well-being.

Humankind is very ill at this crucial time in history, when we could be on the brink of destruction. At the time of writing, the US President is seeking a mandate from the world leaders to invade Iraq. Why do we choose leaders who are so lacking in wisdom? How could we all be so stupid? Have we not yet heard that causing suffering only breeds more suffering. Hasn't September 11th healed any of those wounds?

Roy's book is a way out of this dilemma. Read it and enjoy the nectar that flows from each page.

Eddie Shapiro
Totnes, Devon
August 2002

Introduction

Why should we be interested in spiritual matters? This is a book which explores the nature of spiritual reality and how we can properly understand and integrate it into our lives. For the reader who is not familiar with such things, I would simply ask him or her to put aside any scepticism (even put aside the word 'spiritual'), because I am not trying to convert or manipulate the reader in any way. If you don't like what you see, you don't have to read the book. If you are quite happy in living the way that you are, then what can you possibly gain from reading such a book? However, if you have questions and doubts, if you have fears about the future or if you feel depressed or unhappy and can't quite work out why, then reading further may help ... but then it may not.

This book is the outcome of more than thirty years of spiritual enquiry, living and working with it along the way. I don't claim any divine authority for the words that have come through me. All I can say is - please read on. There is a certain amount of repetition of ideas and phrases throughout the various chapters, but hopefully this repetition will have a reinforcing effect - clarifying what is written. The book was not written merely as an intellectual exercise, but from what I term 'the feeling'. Intellectual understanding of spiritual matters, in my view, has only limited value. I often use the phrase "from the silent emptiness of our true nature", because this phrase sums up for me the level at which our understanding needs to become established.

The principal approach of this book is that of Advaita (non-dualism), about which a little more explanation is given in the first chapter. There is an enormous interest in Advaita at the time of writing, but I feel that few authors of books on Advaita effectively deal with how to actually put it into practice in daily life. Hopefully, this book goes some way towards redressing this situation by encouraging the reader to take Advaita philosophy out of the book and into daily life situations.

I have used, for the most part, everyday language that highlights aspects of life as most of us experience it. For the Advaita aficionado, I apologize for not always keeping faith with non-dual advaita-speak. I don't feel that it is possible or worthwhile trying to make sure that every word and sentence conforms strictly to the unwritten canon of Advaita. More important is how we live it.

For readers who may be interested, my three prime influences along the way have been (in chronological order) J.Krishnamurti, Nisargadatta Maharaj and Jean Klein. Whilst Krishnamurti and Nisargadatta are rightly popular and widely acknowledged, I would also suggest to interested readers that they seek out the writings of Jean Klein, whose clear and subtle expression is in my view unsurpassed amongst the many teachers of

Advaita. Those who were fortunate enough to have had close association with him will remember him with enormous love and respect.

I hope that your journey through this book will be stimulating and enlightening. However, please do not view it as a book of ideas that can be skimmed through like one would skim through a novel. Open it anywhere, take a short section and read it in reflective mood. More than anything, it is a book of perspectives, exploring the limitations of 'ordinary' life in the context of life as a whole. What becomes of our aspirations? Who are we? How can we find liberation from confusion and suffering? These are questions that most of us might ask at some stage in our lives.

I see this book as a picture in words - a picture of the great play of life. I also acknowledge that there are many other ways of painting such a picture. Nothing is fixed in reality. The play unfolds as it will. All we can do is go with it. Fighting against it is what causes us grief and suffering. Arguing over words and definitions is a pointless and unhelpful exercise, as can easily be seen from a simple study of history.

Roy Whenary
Totnes, England
August 2002

Chapter 1

LIVING ADVAITA

Our apparent separateness
from the rest of the universe
is not due to the universe
being separate from us,
but because we have
contracted within our minds
what we think we are.

Advaita (meaning 'not two' in Sanskrit) is not a difficult philosophy to begin to understand intellectually. It is a non-dualistic perspective and outlook on life, which reveals the fundamental underlying unity of all things, and is realized through direct experience. Reading a few books on the subject should clarify for most people, what the basic approach is. However, intellectual knowledge about Advaita is only the first step towards a more integral understanding.

Advaita is known as the Direct Path, because it does not get bogged down with philosophical and theological issues. Instead, it approaches reality directly, free from concepts. This it does by abandoning the intellect beyond a certain point in the enquiry. Of course, this approach is not confined to the world of Hinduism and Advaita, but is clearly visible in the Dzogchen teaching of Tibetan Buddhism, in Zen, Sufism, Taoism and in many other traditions.

Advaita takes us beyond subject-object duality, where there is no observer to observe a world of objects outside of itself. The observer and the observed become one. The mind no longer separates itself from the world that it inhabits, but relates in a more integral way with it. In reality it is all in the seeing. When the mind no longer isolates itself from the world, it begins to experience the world more on the level of feeling than intellect. This opens up a whole new way of Being.

Underlying everything that we think we are, there is a basic oneness that we share with all creation. This is often referred to as 'our true nature'. But it is not an object like any other object. It is ungraspable and indefinable, and yet it is the fundamental ground of our Being. It is our essence, our spirit of oneness with the universal.

The intellect can never understand what our true nature is. If we don't step out of the intellectual prison, we can never know what freedom is. The intellect functions always within the realm of what is already known and stored in memory. This means that it can never be fully creative or explore what might be beyond the bounds of what it knows or believes.

Our apparent separateness from the rest of the universe is not due to the universe being separate from us, but because we have contracted within our minds what we think we are. We have identified with the particular, the small, the personal, the individual and we have pushed away, in our minds, everything that goes beyond that limited perspective.

This attitude has isolated us within a virtual world of our mind's own making. It is the prison from which we strive all our life to break free. One of the ways in which we learn to break free is by listening to others who have done so. Of course, these so called 'others' are not separate from us. They appear in our human vision to be physically outside of us, but in reality they (the teachers and the teachings) are not separate from us. They carry the resonance of our common true nature and stimulate the awakening of our inner intelligence.

Subject and object are passing apparitions. They appear to be separate, but only in time-bound awareness, in duality. In the Advaita approach we go to the core of what we are, to the essence, which is not the creation of the intellect, and cannot be grasped by the acquisitive mind. It is also not the realization that comes at the end of a process, so there are no devised methods, no rituals, to take us there - because 'there' is not somewhere outside of ourselves, in some other place in time and space.

3

We cannot grasp what we already are - we can only Be it. That which grasps and that which is grasped are not what we truly are. This we can only realize in the silent emptiness of our true nature. But even to say that we are 'our true nature' or 'consciousness' is to objectify what we are - which is to deny it. This is why we must take our understanding deeper, to the feeling level, and not try to capture it with the mind.

We must always be aware that our use of language is limited, is only representational. Krishnamurti used to say "the word is not the thing", a table is not the word 'table'. The word is only a symbol, something which hints at something else, but cannot fully convey the meaning or significance of it. So, we must be careful not to get trapped in words and definitions.

We must be careful not to become hypnotized by words. Every teacher uses his or her own particular language. We never reach the heart of a teaching by hanging onto the words, imitating the words and thinking that we understand everything from those words. When we really understand, we begin to use our own language, our own expression - we no longer stick to formulas and phrases that our teachers used.

Spiritual understanding is not something which comes from the head, from the intellect - it comes from a deep feeling-level understanding. It is something which we contact, or touch, with our whole being, because it is not separate from us. And when we touch it with our whole being, the way that it expresses itself is through the language that is natural and particular to us.

There are times when it is necessary to go away from the world, to retreat and go deep into oneself in a quiet environment. However, the real challenge is to live in the world with ordinary people - with anger, fear, desire and all the emotions going on around one. How do I respond to these emotions? Do I put up a wall, do I react, do I become aloof?

It is easy to sit on the top of a mountain, breathing the fresh air, taking in the vast panorama, and thinking that one has got it. It's great to stand on the seashore watching the sun going down, with no cares in the world. But the test is in living in the world, working to pay the rent or mortgage, bringing up the children, struggling with the finances - and still being able to live the understanding at a deep feeling-level.

This is not to say that one has to do all this. Everyone's situation is different. But there is a need for challenge. Otherwise, the understanding may be only in the head. One may even be able to convince others that one has really got it, even though one may have always avoided challenging situations.

In living Advaita, we are no longer pushed and pulled by the emotions. We stand back, not because we are fearful or want to be in control, but because we are no longer hypnotized by what is apparently going on around us. In living Advaita, we no longer see the world in terms of 'myself' and others - we no longer live the subjective life, in that sense. Instead, we live more from emptiness, from silence, from our true nature, and the 'person' that we have always thought ourselves to be, takes a back seat.

There is nothing extraordinary about this. This is how we can all live, given a certain amount of inspiration and direction. The whole concept of 'self', which society very much believes in, is based on the illusion of permanence. We see ourselves as permanent, separate and distinct individuals, even though life, spiritual traditions and modern science tell us otherwise.

The body-mind that we think we are is a continuously changing and evolving energy system that is anything but permanent, separate or distinct. There is in fact nothing fixed about it. After sixty, seventy or one hundred years everything finally and totally falls apart anyway. We spend our whole life accumulating experience, possessions, wealth, fame, and then we are nothing. So there is nothing at all permanent about us.

Advaita is very clear from the start, that 'I' as a person, as an individual, am an illusion. Now, this doesn't mean that 'I' am not a living manifestation of the One Universal

Life. It simply means that I need not get caught up in believing that I am something which I am not. In staying with the understanding of what we are not we can truly be what we are. This is what liberation is about - liberation from the illusion that we are a something and a somebody.

The language of non-duality is very easy to play about with. The challenge is to live it. No one is more special than anyone else. Given the right tools, it is easy for anyone and everyone to begin to unfold from within themselves the truth of their true nature, to actually live this Advaita philosophy. It is something very down to earth, simple to understand and not difficult to implement, if one is earnest not to live in limitation and suffering.

We have all been conditioned for so long into believing that we have no power, that we need to obtain it out there in the world, in our bank account, in our car, our job, our house, our status in society, our experiences in life, from our guru, and it is not so easy for us to psychologically break free of this strong and sustained conditioning. The simple teaching from Advaita is that there is no need to break free, because we are, in our essential nature, already free.

You are not who you think you are - a limited bodymind

mechanism existing in isolation from everything else. You are, in yourself, the essence of life. You are the wind blowing through the leaves of the trees; you are the fire in the volcano, the stream coursing its way through the narrow valley, the earth rising up to meet the sky in the form of a tree or a flower; you are the rock of ages. Yet for now you are also a man or a woman, exploring for a while the limitations of humanity, thought and the power of love and truth to take you beyond your temporary human condition.

Never think for a moment that you are merely a bank clerk or an electrician. These may be what you do, but inside and beneath all this, you are completely without limitation, free - for now and all eternity. To believe otherwise is folly.

Chapter 2

THE TEXTURE OF BEING

It is with the 'feeling' that we truly
understand and comprehend.
The mind understands very
little, because it is usually
disconnected from reality.

We can, as an occasional experiment, stop what we are doing at any moment to just be receptive, to listen, to look and to feel the silent emptiness out of which all activity springs. We can become aware of our thinking, active, mind and stand back from it, let it rest in the silence, open our eyes to the vibrancy of each moment. If we can take the time to be receptive in this way, we become aware that there is an aliveness pervading the very air that we breathe, every thing that we see, hear and feel, and we become aware almost of the very texture of Being itself.

Some people call this meditation. Others call it contemplation. But we don't necessarily need to formally practice it at regular times in our life, for it is there awaiting our presence whenever we remember to simply stand back from our activities.

As we become more and more familiar with being receptive in this way, we find that our thinking process naturally begins to convert to a feeling process. By 'feeling' we are not talking about emotion, but a more tactile sense in which we 'feel' things at a body level, in the nervous system. It has nothing to do with 'my feelings', and there is nothing personal in all this. It is not something that I can claim ownership of or personal credit for. It just is.

'Going into the feeling' is an expression that describes how it is possible to live the non-dualistic life. This is not only an idea - it is something that each of us can experience here and now. If it remains just an idea, then it means absolutely nothing. We take the experiences of every day, every moment, and bring them into the body, into the feeling. It is with the 'feeling' that we truly understand and comprehend. The mind understands very little, because it is usually disconnected from reality. It has its own script, which just keeps running despite what happens around it. In 'feeling' something, we are being fully receptive to it, we accept it, we listen to it completely, we taste its flavour and smell its perfume.

When someone is angry with you, feel the vibration of that anger, listen to it, get to know it, don't condemn it, don't shy away from it. What does it feel like for you? Do you feel hurt or fearful in its presence? Just become acquainted with what you feel in the presence of anger.

When desire or fear arise in you, just watch what is happening, see where they are coming from and what results from them. What do they feel like in your body? What happens to them when you breath out and in several times? In going into the feeling, in all situations, with everyone and everything that one comes into contact with, soon one finds that one is standing back from life rather than pushing oneself forward into it. One is beginning to listen to what life has to say, to receive experiences fully and to move closer to an integral understanding of life rather than living from a disconnected intellectual perspective or from a perspective that is merely reactive.

In going into the feeling, one's emotional being is informed differently to the way which society encourages. When you are living from the feeling, you are no longer pushed and pulled by emotion. You are not grasping after results or desperately seeking acknowledgement or approval from others. You are not living in fear of what others think or say. In going into the feeling you are standing back from personal involvement. You are not running away from responsibility, but taking responsibility for your own feeling. This is a different way of relating to life. It is an impersonal way of relating to life, but it is also deeply personal to the core.

In living from the feeling, one is truly awake, fully conscious. Everything is seen, everything is felt, life flows without any sense of inhibition or restriction. But the world is always seeking to pull you in, tie you up, take you away from the feeling, lead you into unconsciousness, into the emotional. This is the play of life - the great illusion. *reactivity*

When someone asks you if you want to go for a walk, do you automatically say 'yes', even though you may be in the middle of doing something else and not quite ready for a walk? Or do you stay in the feeling and say precisely what you are feeling, which may be that 'yes' you would like to go for a walk but only after finishing what you are in the middle of doing? Quite often we may simply adjust to what others want simply because we want to please, for whatever reason, or because we may feel lonely on our own.

In staying with the feeling, not just in simple situations like this but in all situations in life, we allow ourselves the possibility of being truly fulfilled in what we are doing. Staying with, and feeling, the loneliness can also empower us. Moving away from the loneliness merely roots it deeper in our mind and reinforces the fear behind our habitual response to it.

As we begin to live more in the feeling, we also become more acquainted with and trusting in the silent emptiness that underlies our often busy lives. Instead of fleeing from the empty feeling, one realizes that the emptiness is the place that refreshes and renews us, that really cleanses our mental and emotional aspects. It is not that we necessarily go into the emptiness as a practice - it simply becomes our new automatic response, and we begin to live from the silent emptiness.

We don't have to force or struggle with ourselves to return to the silence when we have moved out of it, because we learn that it is good for us, that we feel alive there and function more effectively. It is like having a shower to cleanse and refresh our body. The mind is cleansed by showering in the silent emptiness. If we shower in this continuously, then there is no place in us for any psychological dirt or dust to cling.

It is important to understand the difference between 'feeling' and 'feelings'. 'Feelings' are a personal, emotional response to life, which is a perspective that is deeply rooted in duality, therefore perpetuating any suffering that we may be enduring. 'Feeling' is not personal. It is more functional than anything. It allows us to gauge situations clearly, without the bias of personal input. It allows us to stand back from personal involvement in situations and to go deeper into the true nature of things. It is a much more subtle level of contact with life, and liberates us from the suffering that is the outcome of living in our feelings, in our emotions, in the personal.

There is, in reality, nothing 'personal' about our life. Through our repetitive thinking processes and our emotional involvement, we have temporarily created this virtual entity that we call 'me' or 'I'. Life knows no 'me' nor 'I' - it exists purely in our imagination. When we learn to live from the feeling, rather than from 'feelings', we truly begin to live a realistic life. Until such time, we are living in a dream - a dream that very soon passes and is gone forever.

Chapter 3

BEYOND THE DOER

In entering into the 'feeling'
of what it is like being a 'doer'
we become more conscious
of the unconscious repetition
of what is happening.

In most of our activities in life, we take on the role of 'doer'. We think of ourselves as some kind of fixed, permanent, controlling entity, capable of doing this and not doing that, at will. Of course, this would appear to be an accurate view of the way things are. The more established we are in our society, the more power, influence, wealth and sense of control we have - or so it seems.

When we say 'I', most of us are referring to an image we have of ourselves, which will be all wrapped up with our personal experiences and conditioning in life, our inherited tendencies, our status in society, our success or failure and our sense of well-being.

We have this image of ourselves, which is unique to our own mind, which is what we think we are - and from this, we act out our life. We walk or push our way through life, wilfully believing that we have the power to 'do', to control and manipulate life into fitting in with our desire to be in charge and make decisions. In this frame of mind we struggle our way through life from youth to old age. But what happens to this 'doer' at the end of a life? What happens to all its achievements and acquisitions?

In reality, there is nothing fixed or permanent about any human being. It is like the computer suddenly taking pride in all the information it has recorded on its hard disk. Whatever it does will always be within the limitations of the operating system and programmes that are installed on it. But the real beauty of the computer lies in its ability to accommodate many different possibilities. Neither the data recorded nor the programmes themselves mean anything more than what they are. The hard disk of the computer is like the silent emptiness of our true nature, which underlies all the content (operating system, programmes and information) of our consciousness. The batteries or electric power are Life itself, empowering us to Be, bringing light to consciousness.

Acting from the 'doer' you are merely acting from repetition. There is nothing new or creative about anything that is born out of the 'doer' mentality. It is an illusory character which your mind has created as a concept in order to perpetuate itself. Question this and fear arises, or anger, to dispel and discredit that which threatens the continuance of this 'doer'. You, as the doer, are always doing things in order to maintain your belief in your own existence. The 'doer' is an habitual response of the mind. It (which you might also call 'ego' or 'self') is neither bad nor good in itself - it is merely a habit.

Clearly, from a spiritual or scientific perspective, there is no substance to the 'doer', to the ego. It manifests in the world for a period of time and then is gone. Even in its apparent life, it never has any fixed point and is continually modifying itself. But, the underlying sense of 'I' that it feels throughout its fluctuating life refers ultimately only to the fundamental ground of its Being, to the silent emptiness of its true nature.

There is nothing 'personal' in all this. Nature, life and the universe do not acknowledge what we call the 'personal'. Whether you are born as Jesus Christ, the future King of England or as an anonymous poverty stricken individual in Africa, you are merely a temporary bubble in the vast ocean of existence. Your story may be quite extraordinary, but ultimately it is of little consequence in the overall scheme of things.

So, what is it like entering into the feeling of being the doer? We need to feel it through in order to understand this in a non-intellectual way. Is there not always a tension and anxiety connected to the feeling of being the doer? Why do we need to sleep at night? Is it not because we would go completely mad if we were stuck in the 'doer' mode continuously, every day and night of our lives?

Without the refreshment that comes from going into deep dreamless sleep most of us would quickly become completely desperate, confused and dysfunctional. Dreaming may continue to unravel the mysteries of our daytime consciousness, but dreamless sleep gives the mind a daily relaxing shower from our true nature. The 'doer' is a contraction, a limitation, a prisoner of the mind. We are fixated by this non-entity, and this fixation causes tension and anxiety in all that we 'do'.

Imagine the quality and depth that comes from a mind that is not burdened by the sense of being a 'doer'. Such a mind flows like water, like poetry. Creativity exudes continuously from such a mind. The sad fact is that we all have such a mind but don't realize it because we are so hypnotized by our belief in 'the doer'. It is as if we have deliberately cut ourselves off from what we really are. Someone points it out to us, and we either dismiss it or agree, but still continue cutting off.

In entering into the 'feeling' of what it is like being a 'doer' we become more conscious of the unconscious repetition of what is happening. This awakens us into more frequent awareness of feeling ourselves as the doer. New patterns become established in the mind, which eventually grow into a more constant awareness, on a feeling level. We then find ourselves nearly always in a 'standing back' position, feeling out each and every situation, thought, emotion and habitual act - not as a practice, but as a real, living, spontaneous wakefulness.

It is important, if we wish to enter sanity rather than insanity, not to make much of our growth into a deeper, more feeling-level awareness. It is a normal, natural development of human potential. The moment that the 'doer' reappears to grasp and own this 'impersonal growth' it becomes 'personal growth' and something apparently special. However, to live from the 'feeling', from our true nature, is nothing unusual or special. It is only strange that so few human beings ever cut through the hypnotic influence of society and the historic past, which prevent us from living from the feeling, from the silent emptiness of our true nature.

Chapter 4

DIVING INTO
THE BLISS

We do not need to search
in order to find our true being.
We already are it, and the mind
which searches for it is the very
reason why we cannot find it.

It is possible to maintain a lifelong interest in Advaita and the philosophy of non-duality without ever really being touched by it, without feeling it at a deep level. Through the intellect one can easily arrive at an understanding of the limitations of the intellect, but then if one doesn't take the understanding to the feeling level, one remains standing in front of a closed door.

Witness the blank faces of those who have followed a spiritual teacher around for years. They know his language, they understand what he is trying to tell them, but they don't have the direct experience, or only have a glimpse of the experience. But, quite often, they are looking for something more complicated than it is. If we simply step aside from the thinking and go into the feeling, and listen with the feeling, clarity follows very swiftly. We cannot grasp the unknown with what we already know intellectually. Feeling is a different, and more profound, intelligence.

Our true nature is not to be found at the level of thought or emotion. Imagine that we can dive, with our physical body, into a warm, yet cool, pool, where we feel completely and utterly at ease, fulfilled, happy and fresh, with no desire to go anywhere or do anything because it is so wonderful being in that pool. That pool is our true nature, which is there in the absence of everything that we think ourselves to be. In the silent emptiness of our true being, there is also a fullness and completeness. In the silent emptiness of our true being there is nothing that can provide us with greater happiness, because we are already in bliss.

Desire, ultimately, only seeks to take us beyond the ego which appears to do the desiring, because everything that is done from the ego, the doer, always carries the flavour of incompleteness and dissatisfaction. So there is always the desire to go further. On the other hand, when we get close to transcending the ego, fear often arises as the ego's last attempt to halt the process towards its own destruction. But, ultimately, we cannot control the process. Diving into the bliss of our true being must be a letting go and not a grasping. It is a surrendering to life, a giving up and stepping back from being the doer, the controller, the manipulator of life.

In the feeling-level understanding that there is no doer, no controller, no person or individual to gain enlightenment or liberation, no one to dive into the bliss of his or her own true nature, the door is open. How one walks, jumps, runs, flies, crawls or trips through this door cannot be determined by the one who is about to go through it. We can only stand before the open door and let life inform us, let life take us in its own time and its own way. There is nothing we can do to move ourselves through the door. Each step we make forwards takes us a step back. At the door to our true being the only possibility is Being - neither being this nor being that, wanting this or wanting that.

We do not need to search in order to find our true being. We already are it, and the mind which searches for it is the very reason why we cannot find it. Abandoning the mind and going into the feeling of each and every moment and what arises in that each and every moment, one stays in the feeling, without reaction, without attachment, without intention, and one experiences that moment without translation into the language of the intellect. This is the level of pure sensation, and it is felt in the body and witnessed by the empty but wakeful mind.

In meditation, one sits with openness, not focused on arriving at a thought-free state nor focused on anything else. Thoughts arise, fear arises, noises occur in the room or outside, eyes open, eyes close - whatever happens, one stays with it for the moment, in the feeling, not trying to control what arises nor suppressing any thoughts or emotions. There is no intention in all this. One is merely allowing the spontaneous to occur by stepping back. There is a lightness about living in this way. Problems may arise, but they are all received from the emptiness of one's true being, and in that emptiness the problem loses its power over us.

What we are or think ourselves to be becomes completely insignificant and meaningless in comparison with the vast, infinite, eternal perspective of the universe. All we can do is to offer ourselves to life, surrendering personal needs and desires, giving in open-hearted gratitude for the mystery of life within and around us.

However we approach life, the only way of entering the sacred, the impersonal, the universal, is to dive deep, to give up all notions of me, mine, attachment, desire and so on. In one hundred, one thousand, one million years, of what significance will all the thoughts, emotions and struggles of this fleeting entity have been? This is you and me - passing little poems in the anthology of life!

The story of life, of humanity, of the universe, is vast in

terms of what we know, of what we can ever understand. Death comes, like birth, and there is nothing we can do about it. Strutting and fretting our brief hour upon the stage of life is really quite meaningless. In stepping back and seeing the play from the perspective of one's true nature, compassion arises for all. Humility becomes one's natural clothing. There is no one, no person, no doer, no diver, yet all is blissful when the mind with all its knowledge, memory and emotional residues stands back and lets go of its hold on life.

1. This doesn't "broke" - why then wouldn't more people "fall into it."?

Why would they even be sitting in meditation??

"I invite you to get out of your own way." ??

2. Does he mean recognize??

"When your hand is burning, you pull it away"

★ "... & then is heard no more ... "

Chapter 5

LOVING KINDNESS

How can I feel anything but
Loving Kindness towards another
being who does not know how to
find freedom, but ceaselessly
causes suffering for himself and
others because of his ignorance?

We live in such a self-oriented world, in which the general sense is that you have to go out into the world and grab whatever you can for yourself. From very early on in our lives we learn the philosophy of 'me and you' - me first and you second, or last. By the time we are adults, this attitude is so ingrained into our psychology that most of us probably find it difficult to actually comprehend what another person's needs or suffering feel like - we are so <u>disconnected</u> from our feeling nature, from our heart. *Children of Nanking.*

At the centre of this disconnection is the erroneous way in which we see the world. It is also taught to us that this is 'me' inside this body and that is 'you' over there in that other body. You and I are seen as separate individuals. We have different bodies, a different genetic makeup and different experiences. These facts seem to support the notion that we are separate and distinct from each other, and on the physical level this is obviously the case - or is it?

The atoms and molecules that make up your body are not personal to you. The tomato or piece of cheese that you ate could just as easily have been eaten by me, in which case it would have been absorbed into my body rather than yours. Both our bodies are continuously changing, with millions of chemical actions and reactions taking place every minute, every second of our lives. The body of today is completely different to the body of a couple of years ago, with all the atoms and molecules of even our bones being replaced by new matter. So, there is very little that is personal about all this. Your body and my body are essentially made up from the same basic materials, and they are not at all personal.

You may suggest, even so, that we are genetically different. But, modern scientists appear to be able to prove that we all have common ancestors. You might say that our education and personal histories are completely different. However, we use the same languages, and languages that are different today may have common roots. The ideas and concepts we use, which have been born out of the use of language, are not entirely our own.

There is nothing original, nothing different, nothing better or worse about you or I. We use the same materials in life. So what is so special or significant about 'me'? Why do I put so much effort into 'my' welfare and enjoyment, and so little into yours - and vice versa?

When we look at life in this way, we realize that there is nothing 'personal' anywhere. We are all a part of the great play of life. Matter becomes conscious through us and then disperses in all directions, only to arise somewhere else - and this goes on continuously on a grand scale. Thoughts arise in consciousness, linger awhile and pass into the great well of human knowledge and experience. A star explodes, enveloping every planet and everything in its path, all living beings with their history, their personalities, their cultures, their languages that have evolved over the course of millions of years - all suddenly undone. There truly is nothing personal in this life, there is nothing that we can hold on to, no security, no hiding place - except in our imagination. *Could I have become a Muslim terrorist?*

When we see life at this level, with this vast perspective, compassion arises for all beings caught up in the great struggle. When we see from this level, an attitude of Loving Kindness pervades our life and our relationship with 'others'. We are no longer hypnotized by the false notion of 'self', and see beyond the apparent separateness of things. We no longer live only from the subject, viewing a world of objects outside of ourselves.

be the vine supporting all the leaves ☺

We have taken a step back, out of the illusion and into a world of unity, of Oneness, in which we are all brief manifestations of the One consciousness, of Life, of the universe. Obviously, we still function as human beings in the world, but we see beyond the apparent duality of physical and psychological existence. We cease to be ego-centric, no longer going into the world grasping everything for ourselves. We also understand the need for others to live, flourish and be happy.

Isn't there a hidden agenda here that has ✿ already decided that Bliss & Good & Happiness are the true underpinnings of the world

'Loving Kindness' is a term used in Buddhism. It is a recognition of our oneness with each other. How can I be angry with you when I understand why you are the way that you are, when I comprehend your suffering and your intense desire for peace and joy? How can I feel anything but Loving Kindness towards another being who does not know how to find freedom, but ceaselessly causes suffering for himself and others because of his ignorance?

'Loving Kindness' is not just an intellectual concept, it is a heartfelt feeling which comes from a transcendent vision of the way things are in the universe, in life. All the philosophical ideas and statements about non-duality are meaningless if they do not take one to the source, if they do not provide one with the vision, the greater view which takes one beyond the sense of separateness, beyond duality. Loving Kindness - not me towards you or you towards me - but Loving Kindness towards all creation, is a sign of the realization of the ultimate non-duality.

We are still in duality as Loving Kindness vs. hating selfishness!)

30

Chapter 6

SEEKING HAPPINESS

When we find the clarity of
our true nature, all the
obstacles to happiness fall
away, revealing an inner joy
which, like a flower, is always
ready to respond to the light.

However inadequately we do it, all of us seek happiness in one way or another. The monk may seek happiness through enlightenment, whilst the dictator may seek it through the sense of power he feels through killing and dominating others. The rest of humanity have thousands of other ways of seeking this elusive prize. Yet how many are successful in their quest? For most of us, the search for happiness is fraught with much frustration, pain and heartache, and at the end of our lives how many of us can say that we have actually found happiness?

Advaita points out very clearly that seeking can never bring us happiness. Seeking implies that something out there, once obtained, will make us happy. How can this be? What is this great mystery? Does acquiring a large house or great wealth make me happy? And how fragile is that happiness when my health declines and I am lying at death's door? How fragile is that happiness when my wife or husband runs off with someone wealthier than me? Happiness is not something that can be obtained, achieved or attained by 'me'. That kind of happiness will always come with potential suffering, that will eventually manifest in some way in my life. The 'I' can never be happy, because the 'I' is the very source of separation, of dis-unity, which is the cause of suffering. When I concern myself with 'my' happiness, it automatically conflicts with your happiness, and we struggle with each other in order to find it.

If happiness is a state which comes and goes according to circumstances, is it really worth having? Happiness should never be seen as an object. It is not something which we can go out there and obtain. It is an inner attitude. When you wake up in the morning, do you scowl, moan about what you have to do during the day or about the fact that you have to get up when you would rather stay in bed?

The moment that we dwell in the negative, resist the flow of life, we have chosen to be unhappy. In our unhappiness we may find self-pity, which adds fuel to the ego. In order to escape the prison of the ego, we may get drunk or do some retail therapy at the local shopping centre, buying clothes or music that we cannot afford - which causes us to suffer again. On the other hand, we could wake up in the morning, leave the past behind, listen to the birds singing, breathe the fresh morning air, take a walk, clear our mind before starting the new day and enter the day willingly and positively. This is just a simple example of how an attitude can affect our whole life.

Negative thinking definitely causes us unhappiness. If you resist life, if you constantly get angry, fearful, self-pitying, resentful, hateful, cynical, you will never find happiness and happiness will never find you. At some level of our consciousness we all choose whether or not to be negative or positive in our attitude. One can blame it on hormones, illness, bad luck or whatever, but at some level there is a choice. Two people will have entirely different responses to the same apparent circumstances, but one may feel that he or she cannot cope, whilst the other sails through the difficulties in a positive frame of mind.

What is it in us which cannot cope? What is it in us which suffers? Advaita teaches us that the source of suffering is the dualistic attitude. The moment that I say 'I', the door to suffering is open. I am then in conflict with every other 'I' in the universe. With good luck, a good education, a comfortable family life and plenty of money, I may feel fairly positive about life. But for my next door neighbour, who may have grown up in a violent household, who may have had a poor education and so on, a negative trend may have developed in his life, and in difficult circumstances he may take to self-pity and suffer accordingly.

When we live in the 'I', in the ego, we are vulnerable to what life throws at us. Sometimes we may be up and at other times we may be down. Very few people sustain a positive attitude in all circumstances. We suffer when we stay attached to negative experience - and, of course, we also ultimately suffer if we become attached to our positive experience. If we could only wake up in the morning and leave the struggles of yesterday behind, then things might be different. But this is not how most of us think. Having said this, the way in which most of us think is little more than a habit. This can always be re-educated.

mystery

When we surrender our sense of 'I' to the silent emptiness of our true nature, negativity does not stick to us. When we allow ourselves to be immersed in the silent emptiness of our true nature, we are constantly refreshed and wake up smiling at the new day.

If there is a difficulty with negativity in our life, we can take the decision not to hang on to it and can surrender it to the silent emptiness of our true being. Of course, this is easier said than done if one is suffering. But then

recognizing

 suffering can sometimes empower us to break free from what is causing our suffering. <u>Ultimately, it is attachment to the concept of me and mine which causes suffering.</u> (With some people, there is sometimes even an attitude of "well, it's my suffering and I'm jolly well going to indulge myself in it and get all the sympathy I can from everyone around me".)

 If one takes it <u>deeper</u>, to the feeling level, <u>there is a sensation in the body</u>. If one stays with the sensation, <u>without identifying it as mine</u> eventually it dissolves. Then, one just lets it go, not carrying forward any memory of it, any ownership of it. Then there is a new freshness. If we can re-educate ourselves to take our suffering to the feeling level, <u>step out of identification with the suffering</u> and simply let it go, we will find that a new dynamic will have been born in us.

✻

The <u>ego</u>, the <u>'I'</u>, <u>can never be happy</u>. Emotional attachment, identification with objects of happiness, resistance and negativity, all deprive us of happiness. In the Hindu tradition there is a term, 'nirvikalpa samadhi', which can be translated simply as 'joy without object', which describes well what it feels like living from the silent emptiness of our true nature. It is a spontaneous happiness. It is our natural state of being, our birthright, which is not dependent on any object. Going into the feeling of every situation in life eventually brings about a transformation in our way of seeing and experiencing life. The mind cannot do this on its own. We have to go into the body, into the feeling, and then we may stumble upon this happiness which is our birthright. When we find the clarity of our true nature, all the obstacles to happiness fall away, revealing an inner joy which, like a flower, is always ready to respond to the light.

Chapter 7

LIVING IN THE WORLD

We need to stand back from
all that is going on in the world,
enter that timeless part of
ourselves and learn to feel
what it is to be alive. Then we
can live in the world if we wish,
but not be a product of it.

In the past, if you were called to explore the spiritual, it may have been necessary to have joined a monastery, convent or the priesthood of whichever religion you belonged to. Of course, that is also an option today. We must all find the way of living that is right for us, given our own individual circumstances and inclinations. But we probably have more options today.

Do we want to live in the world, earn a living, raise a family, have relationships and so on, or do we wish to live a more reclusive existence, have few responsibilities and be cut off from society at large? Our answer may be different at different stages of our life. We may also prefer to live in the world and take occasional retreats.

But, whatever we do, it is important to understand our real needs at a deep level.

Whilst at the deepest level we all share an essential Oneness, nevertheless, we do also live temporarily in the world of duality and do have different skills, talents and creative abilities to express and share. However, the task before us is how to live and function physically in the world of duality whilst also residing psychologically and at a feeling-level in the non-dual.

Living in the world, it is not always easy to stay consciously in our true nature without getting caught up in all the activity, the emotional pulls, the ties and responsibilities. Sometimes we may feel like just getting out and escaping to the middle of nowhere. At other times, we may get completely involved in what is going on. Whatever happens, living in the world, our senses are continuously battered by all the activity, all the business of modern life.

Television, radio, newspapers and the internet are all bombarding us every day with news, information, advertising, lifestyle programming and the like. Our senses are filled to the brim with this constant flow of information and influence on our lives. If we have children, it is hard to know how to protect their innocence in a world of mass education and mass conditioning. Then the so called experts tell us we should be living like this or living like that, eating this and not eating that, believing this and complaining about that.

All of this is taking us further and further away from our true nature, further and further away from feeling life at a deep level, and more and more into trivial thoughts and emotions. This is the consumerist society, where we consume all that is offered to us, where society consumes us and then spits us out at the end of our useful life. As long as we throw ourselves into this way of living we will never find happiness, we will never be at peace within ourselves.

We need to stand back from all that is going on in the world, enter that timeless part of ourselves and learn to feel what it is to be alive. Then we can live in the world if we wish, but not be a product of it. Whatever society is today, it will change. All cultures and civilizations have a limited life span and what is fashionable at one time is unfashionable at another. But underlying all that goes on in the world, our true nature is always there, underlying our sense of who we are.

We are never apart from our true nature, except psychologically, whilst we believe in the play that is being enacted in the world, whilst we identify with it and immerse ourselves in it. But we always have, if we are aware of it, the option of standing back and going into the silent emptiness of our true nature. If we don't take this option, then we get swallowed up by the world and all the meaningless activity, and thus miss the plot entirely.

It is a real challenge to live in the world, especially today. Modern communication and information resources mean that we can very easily and quickly gain access to vast amounts of information and knowledge about absolutely everything, including spiritual teachings. The information available to us is so vast that we could easily become confused by what is on offer. But are we information machines? What is the sense of having all this information if we do not know ourselves, if we are not deeply in touch with the core of our being?

The positive side of living in the world is that, if we have at all been awakened spiritually, we are constantly challenged by daily living, by the attitudes of those around us who are completely oblivious to the spiritual dimension. We are continuously challenged to re-think and re-explore our own attitudes - our anger, fear, desire, self-pity, resentment, greed and so on. We are bombarded with so much information and so many emotionally charged situations, which come at us at such a fast rate, that we make mistakes more frequently and more quickly than would be the case were we living in isolation from the world. But we also have more opportunity to observe these mistakes and move on more quickly - if we are fortunate enough to not be completely pulled in by the world and all the activity.

There are many obstacles to spiritual unfoldment in the modern world, but there is also an intensification of any awakening that begins to take place, because the chasm between what is going on in the world and the spiritual perspective is so vast that everything becomes clear and obvious.

When we live from the silent emptiness of our true nature, all the activity in the world cannot dislodge us from that reality. All the armies of Mara cannot force us from under the Bodhi Tree, when we live in the light of our true nature. We may sometimes face the anger and aggression of people we work with, or even members of our own family, but we stay in the feeling, not resisting - listening, receiving, but not discarding, not pushing away, not fearing. We stay in the silent emptiness of our true nature.

Everything that happens, that confronts us in the world, is a part of the great cosmic play of life. Resting in the silent emptiness of our true nature, we watch it flow, neither pushing it away nor pulling it near. People may say that we lack feeling, that we give no response, but what they are really saying is that we do not get emotionally involved, which is what they want us to become.

People use emotion in order to avoid really going deeply into the feeling. It is much easier and safer for the ego to play around with emotion, manipulating other people through emotional blackmail, but never really going to the root of the problem, never seeing beneath the surface of life. But this is what living in the world is all about - facing the challenges, exploring the relationship between the real and the unreal, standing back and diving deep into the bliss of one's true nature and laughing in the face of the world.

Chapter 8

DEATH AND SLEEP

Time is a human invention.
When we live by the clock,
we miss the passing moments
of life, which means that we do
not live at all. These passing
moments are all that we have,
The rest is merely a dream.

Whatever happens in our lives, whatever we make of ourselves, whatever fame, power or wealth we accumulate, there is always death. This world, our world, is a passing dream. Whatever high philosophy we align ourselves with, whatever principles we stand by, if they are not deeply integrated into our actual living experience of life, they are but empty words that will simply vanish without trace in this vast ocean of existence.

So much energy is expended by human beings, on survival or in seeking greater psychological security. If one lives in the third world, the need to find food, clothing and shelter are obviously a priority. In the affluent 'western' world, people are concerned with other things. They are concerned with whether or not they will be comfortable and secure in their old age. The more that one accumulates, it is felt the safer one will be from becoming a victim of a system that treats people merely as annoying statistics once they are past their time of usefulness. So we often sacrifice our youth, putting everything aside for old age.

But, what we try to preserve we will lose, and what we try to avoid, we will be forced to face, someday. Life has a way of making us look at what we don't want to see. The large house, the bank balance, the memories, will mean nothing when we are maybe on our own, old and lonely, having lived for seventy or eighty years, and still out of touch with who and what we truly are.

Whatever happens in our life, one way or another, our whole individual story will come to an end. There is nothing we can do to change this fact. Death and rebirth are a reality which is taking place in us every day, hour, minute and second of our lives, as our bodies and minds undergo a continual modification. Life is not the solid reality that most of us suppose, seduced as we are by the apparent reality that our senses perceive from the limitation of their physical and conditional structures.

The obsessive focus that each of us puts on our own individual, personal circumstances could be seen, ultimately, as a waste of potential. There is no way in which we can preserve, sustain, maintain or perpetuate our self-image, any more than we can build a permanent structure in sand. Everything that we accumulate in terms of power, wealth, fame and experience will become undone before very long. The dream that we pursue has no reality other than in this brief moment in time - and time is an illusion invented by the human mind to support the belief in a solid, enduring world.

Stand back and consider all the billions and billions of stars and galaxies throughout this vast and unending universe. What is time? What is a year, a month, a day, a minute, a second in relation to this timeless wonder? And who are you? Who is anybody in relation to the timeless reality of the universe?

You are personally going nowhere with all your efforts. Any fame, any wealth, any power that ever comes your way, will soon pass. That is the beautiful thing about life - it is forever renewing and re-inventing itself. Every egomaniac dictator who ever lived was blind to the fact that life has all the tools it needs in order to dispatch him with ease. Your dream is not reality.

Only when you live from the silent emptiness of your true nature are you living in harmony with the reality of life, of the universe. Then you do not make yourself out to be anything at all, then you do not spend all your time pursuing money, experiences, power and fame. If they come to you, you accept them, but they remain meaningless to you, because the only enduring reality lies in the silent emptiness of your true nature.

Time is the dream. Time is a human invention. When we live by the clock, we miss the passing moments of life, which means that we do not live at all. These passing moments are all that we have. The rest is merely a dream. If we miss the passing moments as they continuously arise, then we are already as good as dead - we live only in the imagination, in the head, and our reality is no more than a series of electrical events in our brains.

Living from the silent emptiness of our true nature, the pain and struggle of life evaporates into nothing. We go with the moment, we die to the fixed time-bound ego-mind and allow ourselves to be taken by the unknown, by whatever life unfolds in our personal story, knowing that it is the play of the infinite, the play of the timeless.

Truly, in this life, we can cling on to no-thing. To be inwardly free of attachment to all things, to all objects, to all memories, is to truly live. With this spirit, we know that nothing is ours and everything is possible. Death shall come to this form, to this person, to you and I. It is the play of life, which throws up infinite possibilities.

Everything that goes up comes down. Everything that has a beginning must have an ending. It is only a matter of time, but life operates timelessly. Death only has meaning in terms of the particular, the individual who is caught up in the dream of a solid, permanent existent entity enduring for all time. Such a view is a complete illusion, having no basis in reality.

From the silent emptiness of our true being, let us add a little lightness into our life. Whatever we think, whatever we do, we cannot add or take away from what life is. Our hopes, dreams, worries, concerns and obsessions mean nothing in reality. They only serve to push us, as bodymind mechanisms, deeper into the illusion that we are separate, distinct and enduring entities. Our experiences are then of struggle, suffering, fear, desire, anger, frustration and self-pity.

However, our inner reality is more joyful than this. We are no-thing, and the sooner that we understand and integrate this understanding into every fleeting moment that we live, the sooner we shall enjoy living from the blissful silent emptiness of our true nature.

When we go to sleep at night, we are not afraid. We assume that we will wake up in the morning. But, if we were to depart this world permanently whilst in dreamless sleep, what would be our loss? We are afraid of death, but we die every day when we enter deep dreamless sleep. In that state, the sense of the person, 'me', does not exist. One day we will all enter this state permanently.

Just consider that for the rest of eternity, you will not exist - not as who or what you take yourself to be here and now. There will be no going back on this. There is no sentiment and no indulgence in personality from the perspective of the eternal, the universal.

Everything that you feel attached to and everything that you own, including your sense of self, will end. When you enter deep dreamless sleep, this is what happens. But you re-awaken, with your memory intact. Then your struggle re-begins. However, there is no need to struggle in this life. Struggle is caused by identification with this bodymind mechanism and all that it attaches itself to. Stand back from all this. This will end. This has no ultimate reality or significance. In deep dreamless sleep, you re-connect with your true nature. This refreshes your mind-body mechanism, freeing it from the tensions and anxieties of the 'person'. If you did not make this connection regularly, you would be trapped in the mind continuously, and the mind is a prison from which you already spend most of your waking life trying to escape.

Chapter 9

BEYOND EMOTION

When we live from the silent
emptiness of our true nature
something different happens.
Instead of life being a continual
regurgitation of old ideas and beliefs,
it becomes a creative exploration, from
moment to moment, of the unknown.

Emotional complexity, feelings and expressions of anger, fear, desire, self-pity, pride, arrogance, hatred, envy, jealousy, resentment, possessiveness and aggression are generally accepted as being normal aspects of human behaviour. Few people question these, unless they become extreme.

In an enlightened world, its leaders and its people would not be so blind to their own inner psychological state as to wage war against each other. In a world where the ego and emotional reaction are seen as normal and understandable, it is hardly surprising what cruelty and atrocities take place.

The individual ego lives in the subjective reality of its own mental and emotional world. Everyone and everything else are seen and experienced as mere objects - distinct and separate from itself. The pain and suffering of someone out of view is of little consequence, from this perspective, as long as the ego gets what it thinks it wants.

When one lives from the egocentric perspective, 'my wife' in effect becomes my property. When she decides she wants to leave me or have an affair with another man, an emotional reaction kicks in to try to protect 'my' interests. I get angry, I stamp around and become threatening or even violent. The ego learns, in life, that in order to get what it wants, anger and aggression are very useful tools, so it uses them in order to manipulate situations to its advantage.

This is what living in duality is about - protecting the interests of the ego. Emotional life is about the ego: "I want to be happy", "I want to have this", "I don't want that". All the emotions revolve around these issues. Films and television encourage the living out of emotional dramas, big business panders to the needs of the ego and schools teach us how to be clever little egos in our lives.

meaningful t/or
purposeful to
whom ? ? ? ?

If we want to live a more meaningful and purposeful life, *or*
then we have to question all this. What is the point of this
little ego struggling and striving all its life to accumulate
wealth, experience and notoriety to then just disappear *may be*
without trace? Such questions need to be asked, but the *unans-*
werable
trend is towards indulgence and escape, entertainment
and having 'fun'. Entertainment and fun are the 'opium
of the people'.

Who is going to question the drug that they are dependent
on providing that they get what they want? So, the
financial elite of the world will always make available the
drugs that people need - the inner drugs of entertainment,
fun, lifestyle opportunities and suchlike. But in living in such
a bubble, we fail to develop the tools to cope with
psychological and emotional challenge. So there are
experts on hand to provide us with drugs and therapy to
help us through any difficulties we may experience.

In all this, we become completely cut off from who we
truly are and live in a 'virtual' world of someone else's
making. We speak of robotics and the future, but many
of us are already living the lives of robots. If we are not
in touch with the silent emptiness of our true nature then
we are, to a certain extent, living robots. If we are not
living with awareness and sensitivity, then we are living
automatically from some other script, from our
conditioning and the influence of society. From the
perspective of the sage, this is not living up to our
potential.

During the course of our lives we are influenced by everyone we meet, everything we experience and all the knowledge we accumulate. In turn, we also influence everyone we meet and everything we get involved in. Attitudes, ideas, patterns of behaviour are passed around within society. We all influence each other continuously. The more famous and powerful we are within society, the more influence we may have.

If we have something to say from the heart, then we should share it with the world at large, because mind and emotion dominate everywhere. Lives and the direction they go are influenced by what is said and what is left unsaid. *What diff can that possibly make if all mind & emotion are gone? What has the so called silent emptiness to do with*

When we are brought up in a particular society, we are *all this* most likely to take on some kind of cocktail of attitudes, ideas, beliefs, patterns of behaviour and suchlike that reflects the family and the society within which we have grown up. When we express ourselves, most of us believe that we are demonstrating our individuality, our originality, but in fact we are usually merely passing on what we have already learned from other sources, what we have become conditioned to believe. There is nothing original or individualistic about this - we are merely doing what everyone else does.

When we live from the silent emptiness of our true nature something different happens. Instead of life being a continual regurgitation of old ideas and beliefs, it becomes a creative exploration, from moment to moment, of the unknown. Then we don't approach each new experience with the old ideas, old ways of looking at things. Instead, we listen to life and allow each and every situation to inform us. This is creative living. Then our influence upon the world is a different matter entirely.

When we live from the silent emptiness of our true nature we are not living from the ego, and we are no longer living from emotion. Emotion churns around within the field of the known, the conditioned mind. The moment you step into the unknown, there is no emotion - there is clarity and creativity - but not emotion. Emotion then comes in as you step back from the unknown and try to relate it to your reservoir of knowledge and experience. Then you label it as a 'peak experience' because it has shown you a new dimension to living that is beyond your normal, ordinary, boring existence.

Getting involved in emotional issues feeds the ego, the sense of separateness that we feel. It keeps us imprisoned within the narrow field of the known - our memory and conditioning. If we are looking to grow in wisdom and understanding, then we must step out of the field of the known, step out of memory, intellect and emotion, and truly listen to life. If we want to be creative, then we must do likewise. Nothing new is born out of the old. We must let the old die within us, then out of the emptiness that remains the new will come into being.

But we cannot orchestrate this into happening. We can only enter the unknown, and see what happens. Life is the creator. We can never be the creator. We can only ever be the channel for creativity to flow through us. Then we are not even there. Then we are not living in the ego with its thoughts and emotions that never give any time or space for the creative to come into being.

Life, for us, is very short really. It is not so much what we do in our life that matters, but rather how we do it. If we do things with resistance and resentment then we are not functioning very skilfully. If that is the case, then we need to either change our attitude or maybe change what we are doing.

Many people get emotionally involved in the tasks that they have to do, instead of treating them merely as things to be done. To be really effective in life, we need to stand back and not get emotionally involved. Otherwise, we disable ourselves from being able to function properly. This does not mean that we are living in denial. It means that we are choosing to live creatively and also effectively.

Anger, fear, resentment, pride, self-pity and so on, do not enhance or add value to our lives - they perpetuate the sense of ego, of separateness. Negative emotions are like seeds within us. If we feed them, they will grow, and eventually they will take us over, because there is no end to the amount that they can grow. Anger arises and is expressed because we are not even aware of it until it arises in response to a situation. Fear comes into being because we cling on to the known and hesitate to give ourselves fully to the unknown. However, if we catch the anger or fear at the point where they start to grow out of the seed, then our awareness of them will minimize the extent to which they will manifest.

Awareness of the unconscious movement of emotions is helped by certain practices such as meditation, body movement, yoga and suchlike. Going beyond emotion is of great value in our lives, because ultimately it will liberate us from suffering and also enhance our ability to live a creative and fulfilled life. Whilst avoidance of emotional issues may not be helpful, excessive focus on emotional issues can become an endless cycle of repetition in unskilful living. *too true!*

Many people who purport to be interested in inner change and transformation cling stubbornly to the emotional path, insisting that it is a path of liberation. Of course, if there are emotional blockages, then it might be necessary to release them. But if we do not take our feeling-level awareness deeper than our emotions, then we will go around in circles, never finding liberation from suffering. Only in the silent emptiness of our true nature can we find liberation.

Chapter 10

LIVING IN PEACE

In order to bring peace into
one's life, one needs to first
learn the art of acceptance and
surrender to whatever reveals itself in
every moment. This means ..... no resistance.

Very few of us seem to carry a sense of inner peace with us. Looking at the faces on any city or village street, probably anywhere in the world, one sees pain, conflict, unhappiness, loneliness, hardness, but rarely inner peace. How is it that human beings can live for sixty, seventy, eighty or more years and still not find inner peace? Why is it not a priority in our lives?

As long as we are seeking, whether it be after wealth, fame, power, love, experience or enlightenment, we cannot be at peace within. Seeking, end-gaining, means that I am this but I want to be that. Right from the start there is conflict in this approach. I am trying to be something other than what I am, or trying to be somewhere other than where I am - which means that I am not staying with what actually is.

The moment that we try to move, psychologically, away from the actuality of life, we disturb the peace. The habits of the mind usually disturb the peace. Silence is a threat to the ego-mind. When we become more acquainted with the silence, the grasping ego has nothing to cling on to. It is the ego which causes our pain and conflict, because it is always grasping after something else, it never steps back to admire the view of the 'now', the present moment.

It is interesting to watch the mind in operation, to see how, for perhaps most of us, this grasping quality is nearly always present. We even take it with us into the so called spiritual realm. Wherever there is a goal, an aim, an ambition, there is conflict between what is and what could or should be. *How, then, do we make choices, if not based on our wants?? ie - 3 etc. Duck*

don't this a want for peace!

In order to bring peace into one's life, one needs to first learn the art of acceptance and surrender to whatever reveals itself in every moment. This means - no resistance. This also means flexibility of mind, body and spirit. But how does one do this? Well, quite obviously, the answer is that we cannot 'do' this. All we can do is to stay with what is, which of course is always changing. It means that we have to learn to go with the flow of life, not being fixed or attached to any outcome. This is easily said, but the ego has other ideas. It is locked into habitual ways of

is not an outcome? peace!

doing things, it is looking for results, it is always trying to get somewhere and achieve something. But this is one place that it cannot get to, and one thing it cannot achieve - not in a million years. So, the solution is simply to let go of all expectation.

It is possible to dull the mind with repetition, with various practices which will effectively slow up and control the mind. But we are not talking here about dulling or controlling the mind. Of course, if the mind is really hyperactive, then maybe it needs controlling to a certain extent. But when you control the mind, you also dampen down its sensitivity and inhibit its sense of aliveness. We are talking about not damping down the mind, not trying to control it, but allowing it to subside naturally on its own, without any restriction, without any holding back. The problem is with 'intention'. If I wish to become more inwardly at peace because I see the full implications, personally and for society if I don't, then I can look into the various factors which currently prevent me from realizing this inner peace. The understanding of these factors will bode well for the realization of this peaceful state.

One of the big questions to ask oneself is, does one feel as peaceful, happy and at ease on one's own as one is with others. Does one feel comfortable with silence, with nothing happening, or does the mind constantly grasp after something to do, something to escape into? Can you live without excitement, or do you need something from outside to give you a sense of your own existence? Are you a slave to the need for stimulation in your life? - because if you are, you will never find peace, no matter how hard you search for it.

When one begins to see from a non-dualistic perspective, one's vision suddenly becomes more expansive. This doesn't mean that one adopts an 'anything goes' attitude. It means that one sees the bigger picture, the bigger story behind what appears to be happening in any given situation. Nothing is taken personally. Nothing is greedily sought. In a way, one just stands back from emotional involvement in situations - which also means that one is actually freer to go deeper into things, because emotional involvement actually narrows one's perspective on a given situation.

Emotional involvement is born out of the ego, not out of the clear light of one's true nature. To someone who is still involved with the ego, this kind of talk may be seen as a cop-out, emotional escapism, walking away from responsibility and suchlike, but this is not the case. Escapism and walking away from responsibility are also ego activities. When we step back from getting emotionally involved we are opening up the possibility of seeing the situation with greater clarity, which means that a more informed individual can deal more honestly and effectively with the situation than would otherwise be the case.

How to bring peace into one's life? One must really see the danger of not allowing peace into one's life. One needs to encourage a greater awareness in one's life, which means that one needs to support the body and mind in that direction, which means perhaps restructuring one's life, habits and behaviour, the kind of impressions that one subjects oneself to in the form of relationships, working and family situations, the food one eats, the positive things that one does to support a change to a more peaceful way of life. So, perhaps one moves to a more peaceful location, takes regular meditative walks by the sea or in the countryside. Perhaps one starts learning yoga, tai-chi and suchlike. But none of these things in themselves will bring peace to a mind that still habitually grasps at things.

One needs reflection; one needs to stop wanting to move on; one needs to become more acquainted with the silence that underlies all things and all activity. Death is only just around the corner. We cannot waste our lives getting more and more pulled into grasping after that which cannot be grasped, because everything falls away from us eventually - nothing is graspable, and there is in reality no one there to do the grasping anyway. Life is too precious to ignore, and when we do actually stop, stand back and consider, in the silence of our true nature, we see that life is more than we ever dreamed it was.

The preoccupation with what is going on in the so-called

world, with the news, the rich and famous, the politics, the injustice, the poverty, the ugliness of the acquisitive mind and the havoc that it has wreaked in the world - all this drops away in the silent presence of one's true nature, where peace resides.

Whenever we stand back and really enter the silence, the timeless, the eternal, immediately there is an unseen link with everyone else in the world who is also present in the silence at that time, and indeed with everyone who ever, in the history of humanity, also consciously entered the silence. This peaceful state cannot be manufactured, but it will naturally come into being when we resolve to deal with the fact that we are not at peace within ourselves - and take away everything that does not support peace in our life.

Chapter 11

WORKING WITH THE BODY

Living in the mind only
is like living in a virtual world.
It may be your personal reality,
but that personal reality is
still an illusion.

When considering the inner journey, it may not be sufficient to work only with mind and surface emotions. Attitudes and patterns of behaviour get locked into the body, and may need a gentle awareness-based movement or bodywork practice to unlock them.

When we move the body in a gentle, aware and open way, free from the controlling influence of the mind, we may enter a state of vulnerability in which any held in emotions and fixed mental patterns are likely to be suddenly brought into awareness. They may burst to the surface in the form of a great emotional release, with tears, anger or fear. There may be a silent recognition of something we didn't previously wish to look at. But, until we open ourselves physically in this way, we may never know what secrets hide in the depths of our being - secrets which may be quietly directing the course of our life's story.

In moving with the body we surrender our control, going into the pure feeling and sensation of the movement. There will be limitations in our ability to move, depending on our age and flexibility, but we do not need to react to these limitations or allow ourselves to be psychologically constricted by them. We will become aware of our breathing, which may seem tight and shallow. But we surrender all our ideas of how we should be physically, and go with the way things are. We do not identify with any limitations that we feel in our body, in our breathing, and we let go of any personal involvement. Then we find ourselves in the pure feeling of the moment.

It is important never to judge oneself concerning what comes up in the bodywork. Sometimes it might release emotional blockages or give us sudden insights, and it is not always possible to articulate these intellectually. Nevertheless, if we stay in the feeling, in the sensation, without reaction, then we begin to create new patterns within our psycho-physical structure. These patterns are then not only limited to what happens during our conscious bodywork practice. They become our natural default response, so that we become aware of the movement of body, mind and emotions even during normal daily activity.

Emotions have an enormous power over us. They are programmed, at a body level, to kick in automatically. With awareness, this cannot happen. The moment that an emotional reaction starts up, we are now aware of it. It may continue to express itself, but we are aware of it. But it is important that we do not have emotional reactions to our emotional reactions. We need to develop the ability to stand back from our emotional state, neither judging nor perpetuating whatever state we are in.

Eventually, if we continue with just being aware of our emotions as they arise, without reaction, then when anger arises, we will find that it doesn't rise as it used to. It won't have the momentum anymore. And when fear arises, when we stay with the feeling, the sensation of it, from the silent emptiness of our true nature, it vanishes before our eyes.

It is very clear, observing many groups where discussion is the only means of approaching the inner enquiry, that it would be very helpful for most people if they were to do an awareness-based bodywork practice, even if it is not done in a group. Without this, there is a tendency to think that words and thoughts are the only way into the divine, when in fact they are sometimes the door which closes down the opportunity of really feeling the divine within.

One must take the realizations of the intellect deep down,

to the feeling level, into the body. They really need to re-inform the body and all its cells and parts. Without doing this, living in the mind only is like living in a virtual world. It may be your personal reality, but that personal reality is still an illusion.

When working with the body, one is able to explore all aspects of life, because they are there, hidden in the bones and sinews of our bodies. All the memories, beliefs, hurts, self-pity, embarrassments, struggles - everything is there, and everything is ready to be released, to be freed up from the positions we have held them in, in our attempt to build a protective wall around ourselves throughout our life. Through the body feeling, as we go deeper and deeper with awareness, we get pulled into the silent emptiness of our true nature. We are not the doer doing this, purposefully weaving a path towards the divine - but in going into the feeling, this naturally and spontaneously happens.

Then we know deep down, with complete clarity, that there is no enduring entity, no person there in reality. We then understand, from the body level upwards, that the world we have inhabited, which is still apparently there all around us, is a virtual world, with virtual characters living out their contorted lives through the mind only.

Meditation can also take us to this clarity, but discussion, meditation and body movement together can be a powerful transforming force in one's life. One thing is very clear: few people have ever come to this clarity through intellect alone - which is not to say that it has never happened, but that a microscope, a telescope and our normal vision together will give us a wider and deeper perspective than just relying on what we can see with our naked eyes alone.

Chapter 12

WHAT IS THE POINT?

What you have now, which
you do not have to struggle
for, which you will never lose,
but which you may not even
know you have, is Being,
in the silent emptiness of
your true nature.

The attitude of many people, when challenged in any of the areas discussed in this book, might be "so, what's the point?". If you have a fairly pleasant and secure sort of life, a good job, a long marriage, your own house, a little money in the bank, nice holidays, children, a cat or dog, insurance and security for life, you may say "what on earth are you talking about? I am fine as I am". However, whenever you think all is OK, everything is fine, life's just as you want it, something happens.

Life does not come with a fixed, permanent, secure contract. You may think that you're OK as you are, then your mother or father dies and for a while you are desperate with grief. Then you get used to the idea of them not being around, and everything seems to be fine again - then the company that you put a large amount of your savings into takes a stockmarket dive. Then you get over all this and you find that your wife or husband has developed cancer. Then they go through treatment and recover, then you find that you have been made redundant because the company for which you have worked for the past twenty years has been taken over and the decision has been made to cut the workforce. Then you crash your car, or another friend or relative develops a fatal illness, or whatever. Life is a continual series of such events. You cannot hide from them behind the false notion that everything is fine and because you currently have a comfortable life.

As the years go by, you become aware that life builds up and life tears apart. There is growth and then there is decay. What you have, what you save, what you try to protect, cannot be saved and protected. The only certainty is that everything is uncertain. If we truly understand and accept this fact of life, then we will not be emotionally hurt when life takes its natural course, as it will. Accidents will happen, people will die, we will lose what we cherish. In every case, we must let go and not carry with us a sense of loss, which may lead to sadness, bitterness or depression.

In one hundred years from now, it is almost an absolute certainty that you and everyone you know and have ever known will be dead - for all time, for ever. So, what are you trying to save? Is there any possibility that you will ever be able to save it? Is there any point, not in questioning things, but in continuing not to question things? As one sage once put it, "the unexamined life is not worth living". It doesn't matter how financially well off you may be, how famous you are, how well-established in society you are, ultimately you have the same options as everyone else.

You may be able to escape to a Caribbean island when things seem difficult. You may be able to drown your sorrows with the very best wines and whiskies. You may be able to go with the most attractive women or men, but sooner or later it will all fall apart. Can you take that? Can you live with that? The gorgeous, exotic looking woman will age, her skin will wrinkle and she will grow weak, wither and die. Do you want to be a part of that? Or do you shy away from looking at such things? This is life as it actually is.

You may not be wealthy. You may not have the freedom to travel and taste the high life. You may not have the security of owning your own home - and you may want all these things, because the pain of the daily struggle to survive may be too much for you to bear. But the point of all the questioning and looking into life is not in order to become depressed with life.

Whatever you gain in life you are someday going to lose - this is a fact that cannot be denied. Whether you are the president of the United States or the greatest, most highly paid sports star or pop music icon, you cannot have it forever. But what you have now, which you do not have to struggle for, which you will never lose, but which you may not even know you have, is Being - in the silent emptiness of your true nature. This is your birthright, and if you only let go of all the controlling, struggling behaviour and look into things more deeply, you will find that in reality you lack nothing, you already have all the ingredients to provide you with happiness, security and peace.

What more could you want? And it can never be taken away from you unless you allow it to be. It is a matter of coming to terms with life. It is allowing your own innate wisdom to direct the course of your life, rather than allowing all the disparate forces within society to push you and pull you in all directions. What you are in your true essential nature cannot be taken away - and, without consciously knowing this, you can never find lasting happiness, peace and fulfilment in life.

If you still don't wish to commit your life to self-enquiry and meditation, what will you do? Of course, you can carry on the way you always have, knowing that sooner or later life will catch up with you - which it will. And when it comes to it, you can drown your sorrows in alcohol or drugs. You can be bitter with life for putting you in the situation, and become a very unhappy person. You can campaign for euthanasia so that you can just give up when it all becomes too much for you.

Any of these options may be fine for your story. But there is a much more simple way - a way in which you will be enabled to live according to your divine potential. Whatever thoughts and memories you may have; whatever resistance there may be in your heart to changing your attitudes, your habits, your behaviour; whatever hurt and sorrow there may be in your past - you can just let them go. You may have to let go of them a thousand times because they keep coming back, but you just need the faith that they are not what you are. What you are is the pure essential radiance of your true nature. This is what underlies the canvas of your life's painting. All the negativity is little more than the dirt on a window, partially obscuring the view.

Chapter 13

THE PAIN OF SEPARATION

There is a vast play unfolding
in our universe - a play which goes
on and on, a play in which all its
actors, like phantoms, appear
and disappear. The price that
we pay for believing in the
illusion of separateness, is
pain and suffering.

When we take ourselves to be somebody, we both create and perpetuate the sense of duality that is felt amongst humanity as a whole. This is why it is important for us to live our lives with <u>humility</u>. The spiritual teacher who gets on the platform and pronounces himself as 'enlightened', or as 'the messiah' or 'avatar' is as guilty as the next person for this. The moment that we take ourselves to be an object in this way, we are into dualistic thinking - and dualistic thinking is responsible for all the pain and misery in the world.

Every time we reinforce the sense of 'I', by repeating self-centred thoughts and emotions - we further cut ourselves off from life. Every time we spend emotional and psychological energy planning for the future and how we are going to achieve, how we are going to get what we want, how we are going to hold on to what we already think we have, we also cut ourselves off from life. The concept of 'separation' is not some far off notion - it is something that each of us practises day in and day out for most of our life. *Seems like he wants us to act like fools - "& I will*

It is time to take responsibility for what we are doing in *Prove* all this. If we understand that pain and suffering is primarily caused by dualistic thinking, by self-centred thinking and emotion, then we need to give time to address the issue within ourselves.

The individual, the person, cannot win, cannot conquer the whole, the universal life. No matter what you do, life will have you, sooner or later. You may hold out until you are old and frail, but then you will be consumed by the relentless process of birth, decay and death. The longer you hold out, trying to preserve your sense of 'me' and 'mine', the longer you will suffer.

Happiness, peace, love and all that human beings yearn for, come only when we relinquish this obsessive interest in 'me' and 'mine', and inwardly surrender to life.

Most of us probably have a deep yearning in our life, but we don't always know what it is that we yearn for. We may externalize this feeling, this yearning, and say that we are seeking 'love' or 'community', when what we really yearn for is our original state of non-separation. What we ultimately seek is to be in touch with our true nature, which fundamentally we are anyway - because, in that, we do not suffer or yearn for anything else.

When we live in the person, when we live in this little 'self' that we carry around everywhere, life brings us difficulties. When we are concerned about our own personal, individual interests, we immediately cut ourselves off from life. When we understand fundamentally that we are not this person, this body, this mind, and that we are really nothing less than 'pure consciousness' itself, then we also know that we do not need to suffer anymore. Indeed, we also know that there is no one here to suffer anyway and that there never was anyone here.

This whole drama of life and death is one vast play within the universal consciousness. We assume the roles that we are asked to act and we never question them. The pain that we feel and the struggle that we partake in, can all end now, instantly. All that needs to happen is that we see what is going on, stand back, stop perpetuating our habitual patterns of thought and behaviour, and simply be who we are, in our true nature - no more, no less.

When it doesn't get what it wants, the ego usually has a tantrum of some kind, or makes a more concerted effort at ruthlessness. People even commit murder, for very small gains for themselves. But these acts are always paid for, instantly. Some people consider that murderers, thieves and abusers of others have got away completely free if they are not caught and dealt with by the legal system. But, no one gets away free from such acts.

The moment that you commit such an extreme act of separation, such as murder, burglary, child-abuse and suchlike, you further cut yourself off and push yourself deeper into pain and separation. You may think you are having pleasure, that you are enjoying yourself, but you are merely trying to compensate for the pain that you feel within - which is the pain of separation.

The greater the pain that you feel, often the greater and more distorted the acts that you are capable of. In a lesser way, people who are not criminals also cut themselves off from life and carry a continual sense of separation by always being focused on the ego, its gain and its interests. Conversely, selfless acts move us further away from separation and the sorrow that is born out of it.

To see the light, we have to rise up above the dark - we have to say "yes" to the light, we have to breathe out all our negativity and embrace the light, breathe out all our sense of separation and surrender to the light. If we hold on to any part of the ego that wants to remain in separation, we'll fall back down from the light and re-experience the dark, with all the pain of separation. This is what is happening in the virtual world of the mind.

In reality, there are millions of physical entities, people, bodies, running about here and there in the world, believing that in their minds they are quite separate and distinct from each other. Then death comes for each of them in turn - the body dies, and where is the mind? It may or may not continue in its virtual world. It may or may not find another body to incarnate in. We don't know for certain what happens.

There is a vast play unfolding in our universe - a play which goes on and on, a play in which all its actors, like phantoms, appear and disappear. The price that we pay for believing in the illusion of separateness, is pain and suffering. The yearning that most of us feel at some stage in our life is the yearning to return to our original purity, to our true nature, to the bliss of simply Being.

In the silent emptiness of our true nature there is no separation, there is no yearning, because we are immersed in pure and unadulterated bliss. We suffer the pain of separation because we will not let go. The letting go could happen at any moment, even here and now -

just one small step for mankind, stepping out of separation and into pure bliss. It is a stepping without stepping, because there is no one who takes the step - for letting go and allowing yourself to be no one, in the silent emptiness of your true being, is the step.

Chapter 14

RELATIONSHIPS

When we meet each other
outside of the mind, in the silent
emptiness of our common true
nature, then our relationship
becomes not one of opposites
or from different perspectives -
it becomes a relationship from
common understanding.

When we are growing up, we automatically develop a way of relating to others, usually based on the models we see around us. If those around us - our parents, older brothers and sisters, aunts and uncles - relate to each other through anger and control or through cutting off and going cold with each other, then we may well learn to behave in a similar way. But, as adults, we do not have to continue like this. We can question our old habits with the wisdom of experience. We are not bound to repeat the same mistakes ad infinitum.

Living in separation, we are bound to come into conflict with others - particularly those closest to us. So what is the answer? The answer is plain and simple - not to live in psychological and emotional separation from others. But how to do this? Again, very simple. We stop habitually focusing on our personal problems, our own personal happiness, our gain, our achievements, our success and failure. But first, we have to want to do this. Our intention is the important factor in all this.

The word 'relationship' implies that there is a duality, that there is one person relating to another person, which of course is what there is on the surface. Here I am with all my conditioning, my behavioural traits, my opinions and desires and there you are with yours. From our different positions we attempt to communicate with each other, sometimes successfully and at other times very badly.

This is the way of the world. This is the way of nations, of the Jews and the Moslems, of the Catholic and the Protestant, of the right and the left, the Capitalist and the Communist. This is how we relate to the people we work with, to our family, to our parents and children, wives and husbands and those we merely pass in the street. Not only that, with each individual we may also develop more complicated ways of interacting. These usually revolve around one of the following strategies: "if you do this for me, I'll do that for you" or "if you let me get away with that, then I'll turn a blind eye when you do this". It may even be offered in the more aggressive stance of "if you don't do this, then I'll do that".

The ego thrives in an atmosphere of separation. Non-duality is death to the ego, so will not be attractive to most egotists - unless it allows them to be the top dog, the teacher. The teacher who takes himself to be a teacher falls into the trap of dualistic thinking. If you have a relationship with such a teacher, you will never bridge the gap between that person being the teacher and you being the student. The only way you can be free in such a relationship is by walking away.

The ego will do whatever it takes to get what it wants, which sometimes includes lying, cheating, deception, violence and even murder. The world is what it is today because there are billions of people operating in this way, creating havoc throughout the world, using modern technology to get what they want - using war, financial control and manipulation on a grand scale. The politicians, corporate leaders and other controlling influences throughout the world take the lead in all this - but we also contribute by giving them power and by operating in the same way in our own lives.

Whilst we feed this way of living, this way of relating, things will always be the way they are. When we see what nonsense this is, when we see the complete illusion that is the ego, and thus step out of it, we will begin to address the issue of how to truly relate in the world.

In my relationship with you, if I am operating from ego and you are operating from ego, we have no chance of finding peace, love and happiness together. Only when we find ourselves together in the silent emptiness of our true nature can we find what we seek in life. It is not that I am looking for something from you and that you are looking for something from me, because if that is the case we will never find it.

When we meet each other outside of the mind, in the silent emptiness of our common true nature, then our relationship becomes not one of opposites or from different perspectives - it becomes a relationship from common understanding. Then we see the beauty in each other and instantly realize that the beauty in the other is identical with our own. Then we cease to try to control each other and, instead, rejoice in each others' well-being and, indeed, our outward differences. But in order to reach this non-dualistic position we must first let go of any lingering negativity.

Anger, fear, depression, anxiety, self-pity, resentment - these all fuel the dualistic ego-mind. Whether it be in a marriage type relationship or the relationship of two work colleagues, we must put aside our negativity, otherwise we have no way of relating other than from each other's individual perspectives. Only from the silent emptiness of our true nature can we ever really meet without conflict.

In the world of relationships, the 'other' person is my mirror. If I see the other person as antagonistic, as unpleasant or even as evil, it is because I fail to see them as they are in their true nature. This is a reflection of where my mind is. Of course, it is difficult in this human life to see the pure being in one who appears maybe to kill and murder dozens of apparently innocent people or one who simply does what he likes regardless of the effect on others in the community.

We need to have human laws which take such people out of society, away from where they can do such damage to others, but murderers, terrorists, burglars and suchlike don't do these things because they are happy, because they are full with the bliss of their true nature. They do these crimes against humanity because they are out of touch with their true nature, because they are trapped in the ego. As long as we ourselves perpetuate the sense of separateness that everyone feels, through living in the ego, then we are contributing directly to the perpetuation of such crimes.

Our attachment to our beautiful, expensive house, our jewellery, or our husband or wife, is what ignites the sense of resentment or hatred that the impoverished, ill-educated criminal feels when he sees us. Of course, this does not excuse his behaviour, and society cannot accept such behaviour. However, our attachment, our pride, our gluttony, our smugness, receives its own karmic reward. When we cling on to something, we must expect that someone else will want it, to try to fill the void in their own sense of well-being.

Chapter 15

TEACHERS AND ENLIGHTENMENT

Listening to the voice of our
own true nature is what we really
need to trust in. Then we need
no outward teacher. The outward
teacher then becomes, maybe,
a source of inspiration and a
motivating force rather than
someone on whom we
become dependent.

When we are living in confusion, in suffering, in the ego, it seems natural to deify or look up to those who appear to have all the answers, who appear to be very spiritual - the gurus and teachers of this world. Of course, they are a real and valuable asset to society and the evolution of mankind, but we put them on a pedestal at our peril.

It may be true that someone who is widely regarded as being an 'enlightened master' has great clarity about life and, in many respects, may appear to be light years ahead of everyone else, but in essence his true nature and our true nature are no different. The person may be different, the energy may be different - but essentially what he is we are also, except that he is conscious of it and we are not. His body will die and his mind will go, just as will happen with our body and mind. He, as an individual, can no more escape death than we can - except that we would like to and he is not bothered.

A truly 'enlightened' master will never tell you that he is great or that he is enlightened. He will never tell you that he alone can realize the ultimate, that he is a perfect master or avatar, whilst you are an ordinary human being. There are people who will tell you these things, who will make enlightenment out to be something exclusive. There are people who will put themselves on a pedestal and encourage you to bow down before them, to serve them, to idolize them. The world is not short of a good supply of such 'teachers'. But do these 'teachers' encourage you to awaken inwardly to the point where you don't need them anymore?

When one goes with such a teacher, one instantly gives away one's power, one's autonomy, and one becomes dependent on their grace, on their goodwill, on their method of teaching. Of course, such teachers do offer a refuge, a support and advice for those who, for whatever reason, do not wish, or are not able, to take decisions or responsibilities for themselves in this life. But if one is seeking 'enlightenment', it is better to go to a teacher who does not have pretensions about his or her status in life. It is better to go to someone who offers you a pure and unconditional mirror in which to see into your true nature, rather than one which is clouded with ego and the spirit of control and manipulation.

We all have the potential to be awake, to be conscious, in the silent emptiness of our true nature. However, there are thousands of us who have studied spiritual writings and scriptures for decades and still are unable to break through the enclosure of the mind, to taste the nectar of realization directly. Thought cannot take us there. No prescribed practices will jolt us into this realization. No book will lead us there. The fact is that there is nowhere to go, nothing to realize and no one to realize it. We have created this myth about enlightenment and the enlightened seer, out of our own frustration and confusion. We have set them apart from ourselves, as something to achieve, something to reach out for, and in doing so have made them unattainable.

Enlightenment is something we have put on a pedestal, knowing that it is beyond our grasp. Even though the enlightened seer may tell us that all we need to do is to rid ourselves of the notion that we are not enlightened, still we are unable to put this notion, this concept aside. So where do we go from here? Clearly, any move we make in any direction is a mistake. So, we stay where we are, fully experiencing our unclarity, our confusion, our frustration. But, instead of indulging in emotional reaction and negative moods, we simply stay where we are. We live our life, aware of our thoughts, our feelings, our moods and emotions. We do our work, raise our family, whilst all the time watching what arises in consciousness. We see the play of the world, of life, and we stand back from any emotional involvement in it.

There are wars here and injustices there. We may work for peace in the world or try to put right injustices that are taking place, but we continue to stand back from emotional involvement. In doing so, compassion may arise in the heart. When we get involved emotionally, there is a personal reaction. This personal reaction neither solves the problem nor allows us to move on. When compassion arises, it comes with an all-seeing awareness of the suffering of all humanity. It takes us away from personal reaction into effective action. This compassion spirits us closer to realization. It takes us out of the ego, out of the personal, into the universal. We are then no longer concerned about personal realization. The realization comes as a natural side effect of the blossoming of compassion in our heart and mind.

It is natural to have respect for those who have greater knowledge, understanding and wisdom than ourselves. But it is also a mistake to get pulled in by appearances. Be careful of the one who stands before you offering sugar and spice. What's in his other hand? Why is he so keen to get your attention? There are many characters in life who have learned how to act in order to get what they want. If someone keeps telling you he is a good man, does it not arouse your suspicion? If someone goes around under the banner of 'enlightened master', do you not have a few questions to ask? Of course, the teacher doesn't always go around claiming that he's an enlightened master (though some are not ashamed to do this), but he often doesn't try to prevent his followers from doing so.

In my own experience, every teacher I ever met who really impressed me deeply, made no such claims. The moment that someone does make such claims, it gives away the fact that they are living in duality, in separation, in the ego. The bigger the guru, the more likely it is that they have fallen into this trap. We take their advice at our peril. Listening to the voice of our own true nature is what we really need to trust in. Then we need no outward teacher. The outward teacher then becomes, maybe, a source of inspiration and a motivating force rather than someone on whom we become dependent.

Chapter 16

WISDOM OF THE ORDINARY

We need to stand back, sit
back and relax into clarity.
What we seek is already here.
Truth, reality, are not at the
end of some psychedelic trip,
not the result of some magical
ritual, but are right here and now.

Many who feign an interest in the spiritual are not only interested in Truth - they are seeking Exotic Truth, something with mystery, something that is stimulating. Then, it is not enough simply to have a guru - you need the guru with the longest beard, the one who performs the most miracles or the one who has the most seductive eyes. Then, when you get bored with that guru, you look for another one who offers something out of the ordinary. But the ordinary is exactly where you find Truth. The ordinary is in fact quite extraordinary when you look at it in the right way. When you look at the ordinary from a subject-object perspective, it really is ordinary - but when your eyes are able to see from pure Being, when there is no becoming, no grasping attitude, then everything comes alive - even the ordinary.

When we live in a contracted psychological space, the energy does not flow freely through us, so we need to get our energy from somewhere else. Therefore, we devise ways and means to do this, such as drinking, smoking, drug-taking, sex, eating, dancing, energetic music and even business activities. There is nothing wrong with most of these activities, but those who over indulge do so because they are trying to raise their energy from a more depressed state. Their normal state is depressed because they have closed themselves off at some level and the natural flow of energy has been inhibited.

For many of us, the closing mechanisms probably begin to function when we are children, or even before. When we live in full openness, energy is not a problem - it just flows through us without any effort. When we abuse ourselves or cling to certain psychological states, the energy flow is naturally inhibited, and we need to boost it by excessive and dubious means.

When we stop, when we allow our mind to come to rest, the world takes on a different light. Everything shines, everything comes to life. Sounds become richer and colours become deeper and brighter. The active mind must necessarily cut out the detail around it, otherwise it would really suffer from overload. The soft, clear, focus of meditation is not available for those who rush around from activity to activity. The body and mind are able to accommodate great extremes and withstand much stress, but the price is the loss of inner peace.

Excess activity pulls you out into a subject-object relationship with the world. The world then becomes functional only and the flower just another commodity. The world becomes a world of objects with you at their centre, using and abusing them at your will. But you also become a commodity, expendable by life, and you pass out at the other end of your life without an inkling of what you have missed. But it doesn't have to be like this.

Stop, right now, and listen. What can you hear? Just keep listening. Sounds will come in and out of your awareness, and you just let them. They are not your sounds, you are not tied to them, you are not attracted to or repulsed by them. They are like birdsong that randomly passes through your awareness. You receive them fully and openly. They may be soft, faint or harsh, but you hear them without like or dislike, and they are gorgeous, beautiful sounds, full of depth and meaning.

Then you look around in the same way, with silent awareness, and the colours, shapes and forms take on a new significance. Every object is a miracle of invention, a living reality that lights up your life. But how come these things seem different now? The reason is that we usually close off and shut down from life, too focused on achieving our aims - grasping, reaching out, looking for the result. Reality is right here, in the ordinary, and we are looking to raise our energy from somewhere else - always out there, somewhere other than where we really are.

We need to stand back, sit back and relax into clarity. What we seek is already here. Truth, reality, are not at the end of some psychedelic trip, not the result of some magical ritual, but are right here and now. All that needs to happen is that we recognize this and stand back from all the chasing that we have done - allow ourselves to receive what life has to offer in the living present. We will never find it anywhere else.

All the seeking that we have done or are doing will eventually lead back to this point of allowing ourselves to be open, to receive life, to be a channel for the pure energy of the universe to pass through us. As the biblical saying goes: "Lord, make me an instrument of thy peace". It is always available to us, but we refuse to accept it. We would rather stay in the confusion that we have known all our life than to allow life to flow freely through us. This is fear - not being able to let go of our control, our intention, our will, our ego, our fixed patterns of thought and behaviour.

Whenever we choose, we can let go of all that - stop, look, listen and receive. We don't need a magician to show us the way - it is right here in front of our eyes. All we need to do is open our eyes and ears. There is a qualitative difference, though, in the way that we see and hear. We are no longer pushing out into the world, no longer grasping or identifying with what we see and hear - we are standing back and allowing all the myriad impressions to pass through us, without judgement, without being attracted to or repulsed by them. We are witnessing life, without there being a witness, without there being a doer, an actor, a controller. We are completely passive in our awareness, and our breathing and whole body function is revitalized, our mind feels fresh and alive again, as it was when we were a child. What more can we need?

Why do we allow ourselves to become so disconnected from life? The world and all its activity pulls us in, out of our natural state of being, into a virtual reality world of the mind. Society, governments, corporate entities, encourage us to get involved in mediocre activities that drain us of our natural energy and our natural ability to live in awareness and inner peace. They seek to make us dependent and incapable of standing on our own. This is not just a problem in modern society - it has always been like this.

The world is the jungle. The vested interests and powerful

forces within society, in the world, secretly control populations through the operation of law, financial control, psychological persuasion, even violence if it is deemed necessary. In fact, this is not even a secret - it is very clear if you look at it with open eyes. But this is the way the world is.

If we are to live in clarity, with inner peace, then we must accept that this is the way it is and know that we can't change it. All that we can do is to not succumb to its influence, not be pulled in by it. The monster, once known, is not half as dangerous as the monster that we do not know. As we change, society will change. There may be leaps and bounds in human evolution, but we only have time to be concerned with the ordinary, the day to day. If we don't transform the ordinary by seeing it with a new light, then change will never happen.

Chapter 17

LIVING IN THE PRESENT MOMENT

If you cannot live in the present moment, there is no other time to live. This is what is on offer - this is your opportunity to manifest your destiny.

If you cannot live in the present moment, there is no other time to live. This is what is on offer - this is your opportunity to manifest your destiny. Your destiny is not necessarily what your mind wants. Your destiny is not necessarily other than what is here right now.

Your circumstances may not be your ideal scenario, but if you do not accept where you are right now, if you always take the escape route when things are not the way you would wish them, then you will never learn how to live in the present moment. The present moment is all that you have, is all that there is, and until you actually learn to live in the present moment, you will forever be dissatisfied, you will never find happiness. Happiness cannot be found anywhere or anytime else.

Living in and accepting the present moment does not confine you to your present circumstances. When your mind is dissatisfied with what is manifesting right now, it wants to take off, it wants to run, to escape into the dream. But the dream does not become reality in this way. The dream, the possibility, the creative unfoldment of your inner destiny, does not come about through the ego's desire and its reaction to the here and now. It comes about through the ability to keep sight of the vision whilst, at the same time, living in the here and now with patient and alert understanding.

Chapter 18

WHERE DO I BEGIN?

Who am I? All I can do is to
Be who I am - to be who I am
in the feeling of it, in the silent
emptiness of my true nature.
I can never say who I am. And
the moment that I say "I am this"
or "I am that", I have lost it.

One of the key phrases of Advaita, stemming from the teachings of Ramana Maharshi, is the question "Who Am I?". But like all oft-repeated phrases, the mind quickly gets used to it and ceases to respond in any meaningful way to the question. The fact is that it is not a question that needs an intellectual answer. Indeed, it needs no answer at all, because the mind can never adequately describe what is felt. Words simply are not enough.

One can stimulate the mind to glimpse things it is not normally aware of, but to create a major shift in consciousness is unlikely simply by repeating a question, phrase or mantra. The mind, or intellect, alone is not the mechanism that can do this.

To ask the question "Who Am I?" we need to really be in a listening, receiving, feeling mode - not grasping after answers to satisfy the mind. But we can also elaborate on the question and ask perhaps, "what is this life?", "what is this Being that even asks this question?". When we look at our life, what do we see?

When someone asks me when and where I was born, I have an instant answer that has been in my mind for as long as I can remember. But where do I really begin? Where did this individually aware consciousness arise? Where was I before my apparent birth, and where will I be after my death?

We live whatever life that we live, for maybe seventy to one hundred years, nicely involved in our own individual story. But what does it mean? In the great vast ocean of existence, what does 'my' life mean? I may be a great sportsman or woman, a famous singer or a roadsweeper. I may be a King or Queen, a President, Prime Minister or famous writer. I may be an enlightened sage. But of what significance is all this? We cannot hold on to these identities.

In terms of the physical universe alone, the ten thousand or one hundred thousand years of human civilizations is as nothing. We focus our lives on such insignificant issues. When we look at the great achievements of Ancient China, India, Egypt, Greece, Rome and then look at our own modern era, what is there that will last? Absolutely nothing at all.

Those names from history that mean a lot to us today, such as Jesus, Buddha, Shakespeare, Da Vinci, Einstein, are like figments of the imagination, passing through our minds into some unknown nothingness. There will be other names, other civilizations, other great leaders in the worlds of art, science and spirituality, but they will also pass on.

What matters in this life is - do you know who or what you are? If you don't know and if you don't even have an inkling about this, other than offering a name and address, then you will spend much of your life in psychological and emotional confusion, boredom or suffering. It doesn't matter who you think you are if what you think you are is only from your memory and imagination.

If you actually stop, let your thoughts unwind and feel the silent emptiness that remains, that underlies all your thoughts and activities, you will come close to knowing who you are. But that knowing is not a thought or a memory-based knowing - it is a knowing that comes from the feeling, the texture of your True Being. Of course, the mind then comes in and tries to clarify intellectually what this is, but everything that it comes up with is short of the mark. It simply cannot be grasped. Even the great philosophers and mathematicians will never understand this simply by trying to create concepts and equations about it. It has to be felt.

When we live our lives in the feeling, rather than in the thinking, we are truly in touch with reality. But there are no limits on that reality, which is why you can never truly say "he is enlightened" - as if enlightenment was some kind of object with boundaries and limitations, some kind of goal that can be achieved or owned. And who is there to achieve or own it anyway?

Do you remember when you were born? It is said that we can be taken back, through hypnosis, to when we were born, and even to past lives. But how far back do we want to go? There is an eternity behind us and ahead of us. What is the point of coming to intellectual conclusions about such things if we are not even present in this living moment? And we can never be present in this living moment if we are continually occupied with our individual, personal, thoughts and emotions.

Do you remember when you came into Being? From where did you arise? When you went to bed last night and drifted into deep sleep, where did you go? When you sit in meditation and drift away from the world of thought into pure Being, pure Feeling, where do you go? No answer will ever suffice. Are you absent in deep sleep, in meditation? Or is it merely that the thoughts, emotions and memories that are attached to your physical form are absent at these times?

We have no way of describing what we are in the absence of thoughts, emotions and memories - other than to say that we are 'consciousness', 'awareness' or perhaps that we are in our 'natural state', in our 'true being'. Words can never describe and never will be able to describe, because words only have meaning and value in terms of duality, in the world of subject-object relationships.

Words can point out the inadequacy of viewing the world dualistically, and thus possibly open us up to being able to leave our thoughts, emotions and memories behind. We cannot, however, step into reality, into non-duality, though we can cease to step into duality. When we see where thought and emotion take us in our life, we simply cease to give them so much importance. When we realize, through living from the silent emptiness of our true being, what richness lies therein, we do not need to try to perpetuate it, because we understand that any kind of grasping kills it. So we learn to live and accept whatever state we find ourselves in, knowing that in letting go of the grasping, we will also find ourselves deeper into the feeling, into the full comprehension of what this life is and who we are. And this all happens without thought, in the silent emptiness of our true being. So, where do I begin? Quite simply, there is no answer worth having. If we look at the elements of nature, does the wind ask where it first arose and does the water ask how it came to be flowing down the stream? Nothing is permanent, nothing stays the same, all is fluidity. Wherever life arises, consciousness manifests. We are this consciousness.

The tiny ant is aware of the boundaries to its existence. Threaten and it moves away. It interacts with other creatures and has some kind of an agenda in its life. It may not have a highly developed intellect or a great deal of self-consciousness, but consciousness flows through it as much as it flows through us. All that is different is the vessel through which it flows and the potential for self-awareness. But water is not affected by the difference in the shape and quality of the vessels which contain it - be they a cup or a leaf. It still remains as water, just as consciousness remains as consciousness.

So, who am I? All I can do is to Be Who I Am - to be who I am in the feeling of it, in the silent emptiness of my true nature. I can never say who I am. And the moment that I say "I am this" or "I am that", I have lost it.

"I Am That" is also a great phrase from Advaita, but as with the question "Who Am I", it can only be truly said in the silent awareness. The true meaning is not in the concept but in the feeling, in the vision, behind it. Likewise, truth is never in the words of the book, but always in the space between the words and the lines on the page.

The reality of what is a table is not in the words, in the definition, the concept 'table', but in the non-conceptual awareness of it. And the non-conceptual awareness precludes the existence of a separate observer of the table. So what sees, what is it that observes the table, or anything? Again, there is no answer. We can only really understand from the empty, from the absence - from the silent emptiness of our true being.

Chapter 19

CONCLUSION

Living from the silent emptiness
of our true nature is the taking
of meditation into each and
every situation in our life.

The conclusion is that there is no conclusion. Perhaps, more than anything, we need to find a way in which we can understand what this life is all about, and then bring that understanding into action in our lives.

This cannot be done through the mind alone. Living from the silent emptiness of our true nature is the way. It is also a jumble of words. If we get caught up in the words, we miss the plot entirely. Living from the silent emptiness of our true nature is the taking of meditation into each and every situation in our life. This does not need to have religious connotations. It is about being fully alive to the present moment, the living reality in which we explore the texture of Being itself - from an impersonal perspective.

If we are serious about life, if we are really interested in learning more about this journey that we are on, we will make moves to ensure that we are able to live according to any understanding that we have glimpsed. Just drifting on in life, without resolving any psychological or emotional issues that we have, is truly a waste of our enormous potential. It doesn't matter where we are in our life story, if we are capable of reading this book, we are also capable of liberating ourselves from suffering by delving into the hidden areas of our mind. Perhaps more than at any time in the history of mankind, there is now a vast amount of information freely available to anyone wishing to find greater wisdom, fulfilment and practical advice on how to overcome self-created limitations and suffering.

Bon Voyage

About the Author

Roy Whenary lives, works and writes in beautiful Devon, in the South West of England. He is also a producer of meditational music.

Roy's interest in the spiritual traditions of the East began in the late 1960s, at about the age of eighteen. However, it was his introduction to the talks and writings of J.Krishnamurti in 1971 which had the greatest impact on his formative years, and he spent many years thereafter attending Krishnamurti's annual talks in England and Switzerland. Then, in 1974/5, Roy came upon an imported Indian book: I AM THAT by Nisargadatta Maharaj, which also had a powerful effect on his outlook and spiritual aspirations.

In 1980/1 he was introduced to a living, accessible, Advaita teacher, Jean Klein, who was a regular visitor to London. In Jean Klein he found a living example of someone who was clearly at ease with himself, and whose teaching came from a deep understanding of both the philosophy of Advaita and the practical application of it in everyday life. For many years Roy attended Jean Klein's discussions and retreats.

Roy has previously published three booklets of poetry (Memories We Cherish/Shadows and Reflections/The Fire of Love) and four of his own meditational music albums (Dawn Awakening/Starlight/Inner Peace/Spirit of the Whale - with Ian Waugh). He has also co-produced six music albums with the composer Robert Nicholas - most distinguished of which are probably 'Celestial Love' and 'Zen River'. 'The Texture of Being' is Roy's first complete book, although he has written prolifically since his teens.

Recommended Reading (a short list)

Jean Klein
Be Who You Are
Who Am I
Transmission of the Flame
The Ease of Being

Nisargadatta Maharaj
I Am That
The Experience of Nothingness
The Ultimate Medicine

Ramana Maharshi
Talks with Sri Ramana Maharshi
Be As You Are (edited by David Godman)

J.Krishnamurti
The First and Last Freedom
Freedom From The Known
The Awakening of Intelligence

H.W.L.Poonja (Poonjaji)
Wake Up And Roar: Volume 1
Wake Up And Roar: Volume 2
Papaji: Interviews

Thich Nhat Hanh
Peace Is Every Step
The Sun My Heart
Touching Peace

Ramesh Balsekar
Consciousness Speaks
Who Cares?
Pointers From Nisargadatta Maharaj

Tony Parsons
The Open Secret
As It Is

Eckhart Tolle
The Power of Now

Thomas Byrom
The Heart of Awareness (translation of the Ashtavakra Gita)

Printed in the United States
29522LVS00001B/121